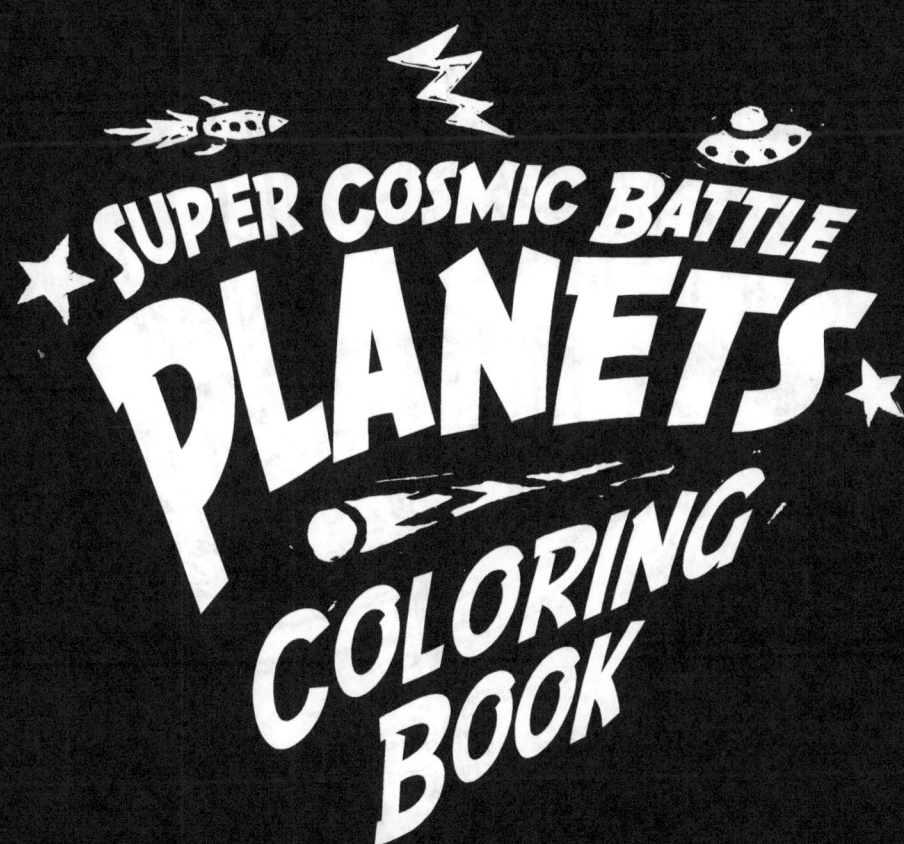

SUPER COSMIC BATTLE PLANETS COLORING BOOK

© 2018 by Jack Wilcox

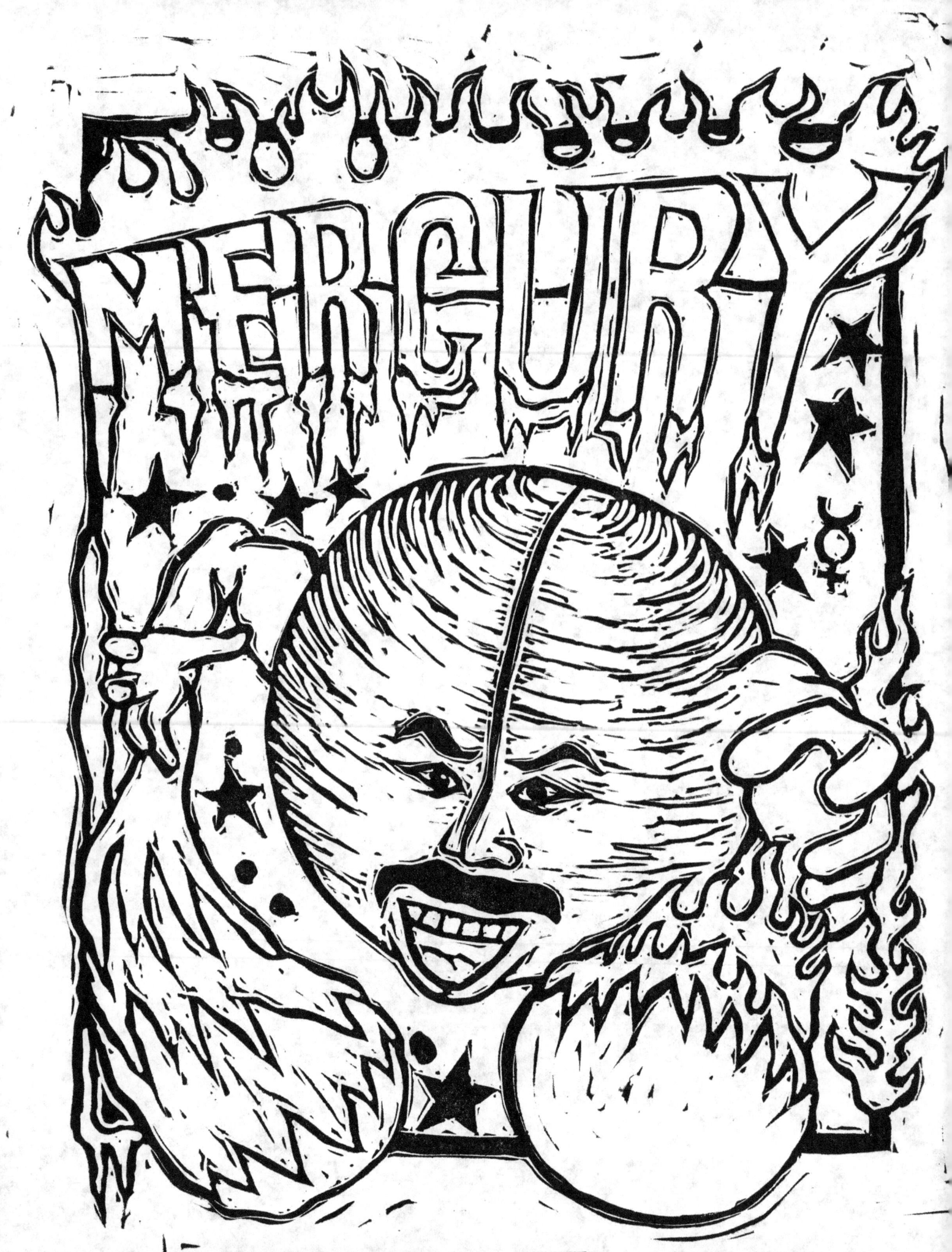

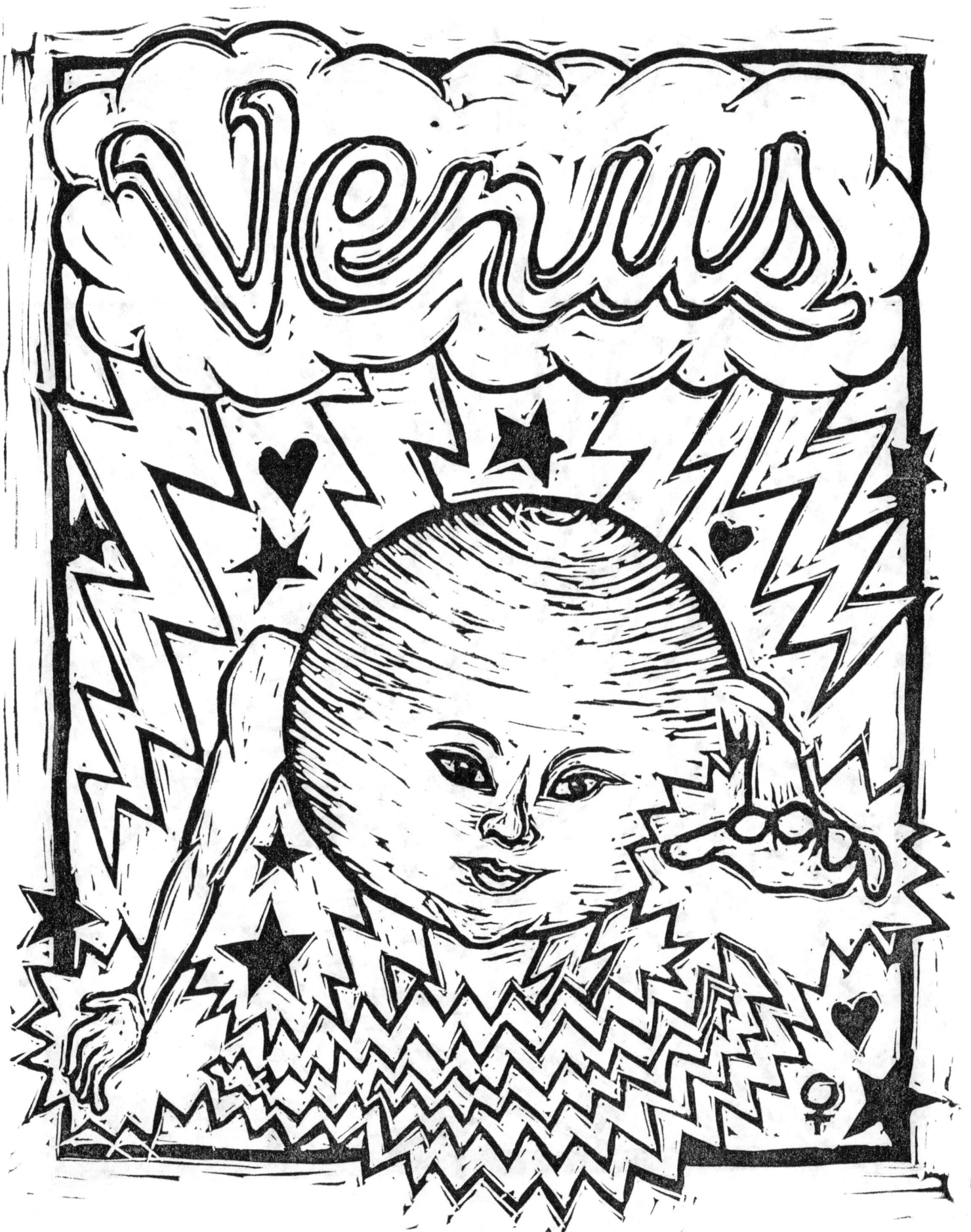

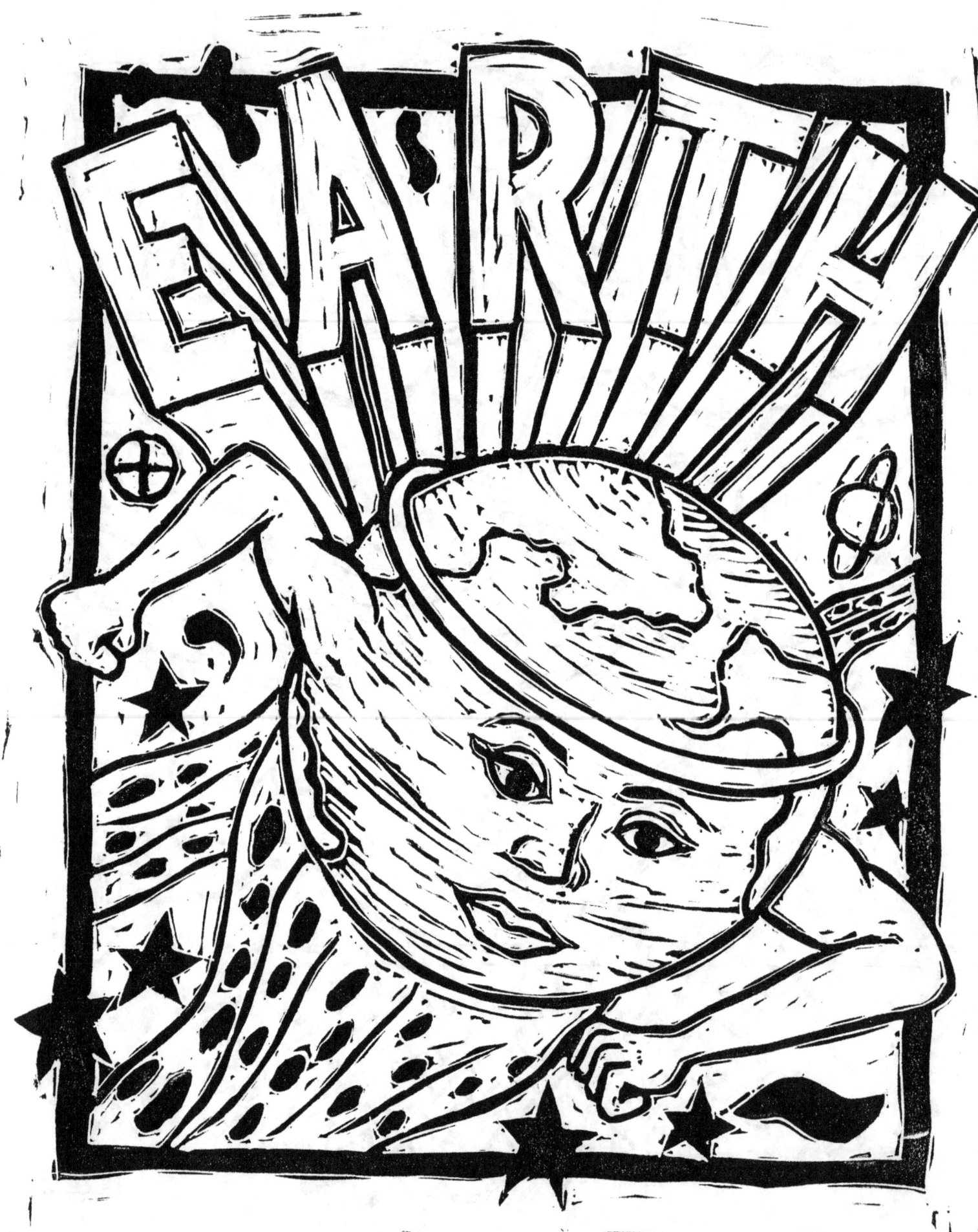

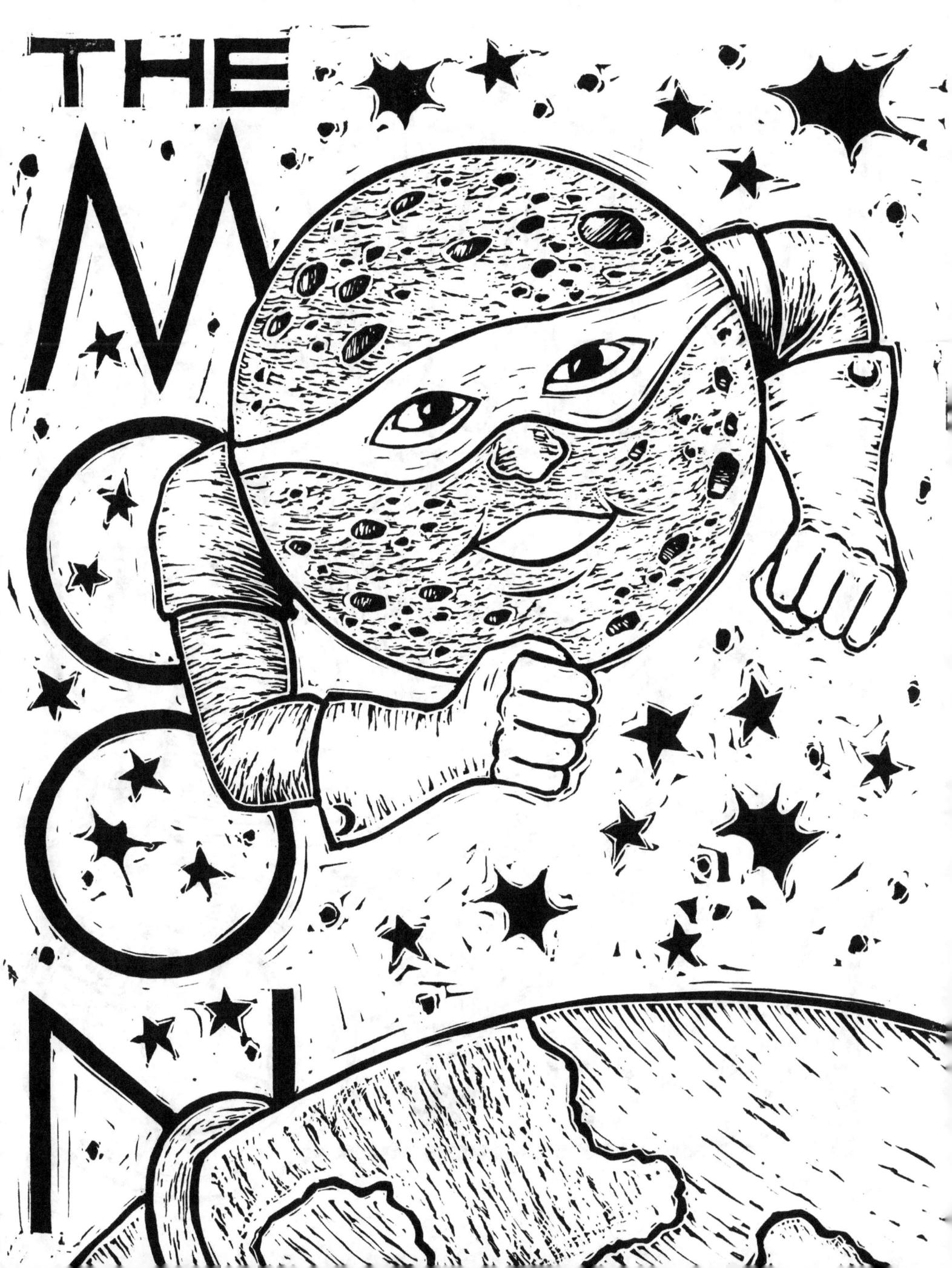

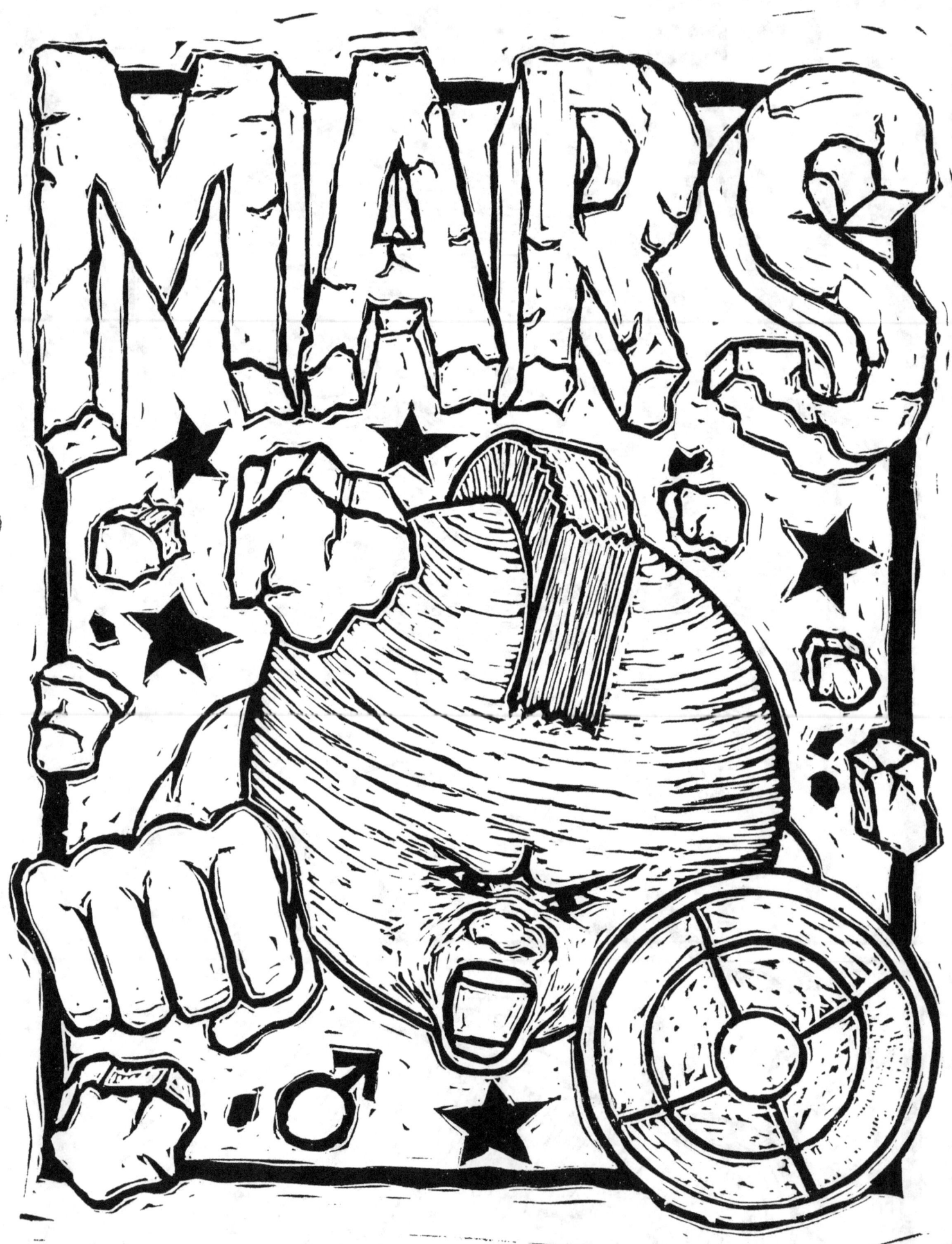

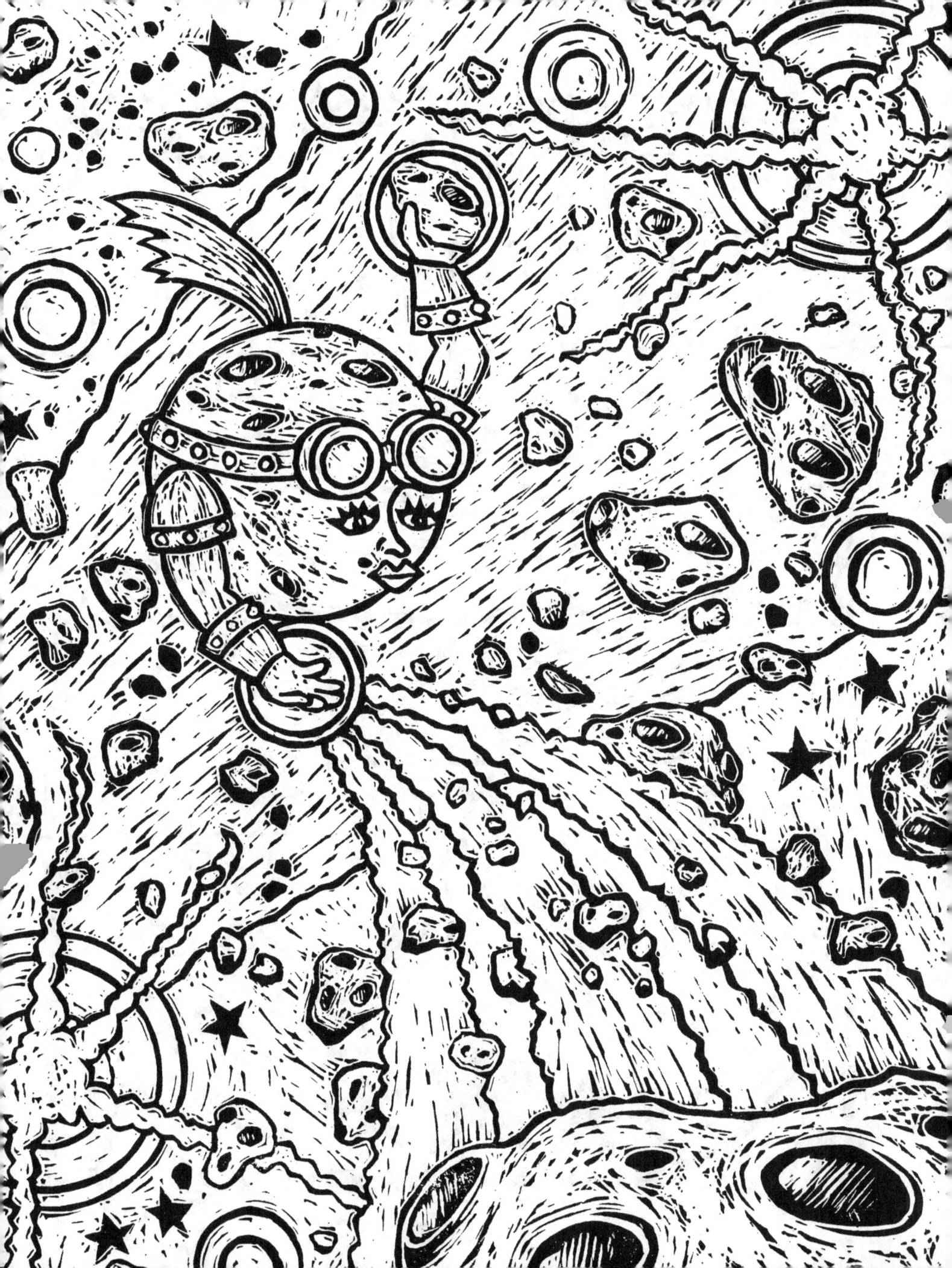

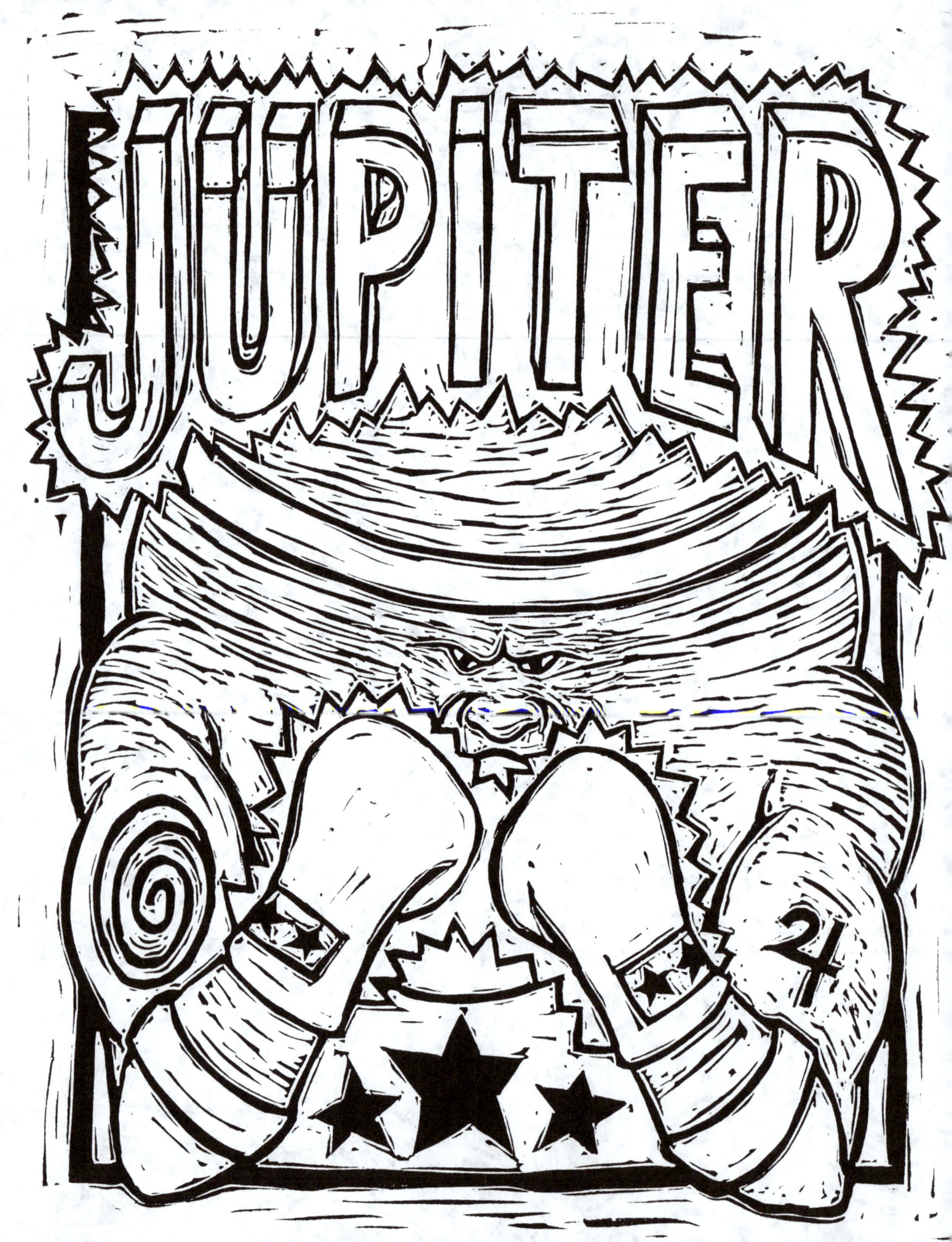

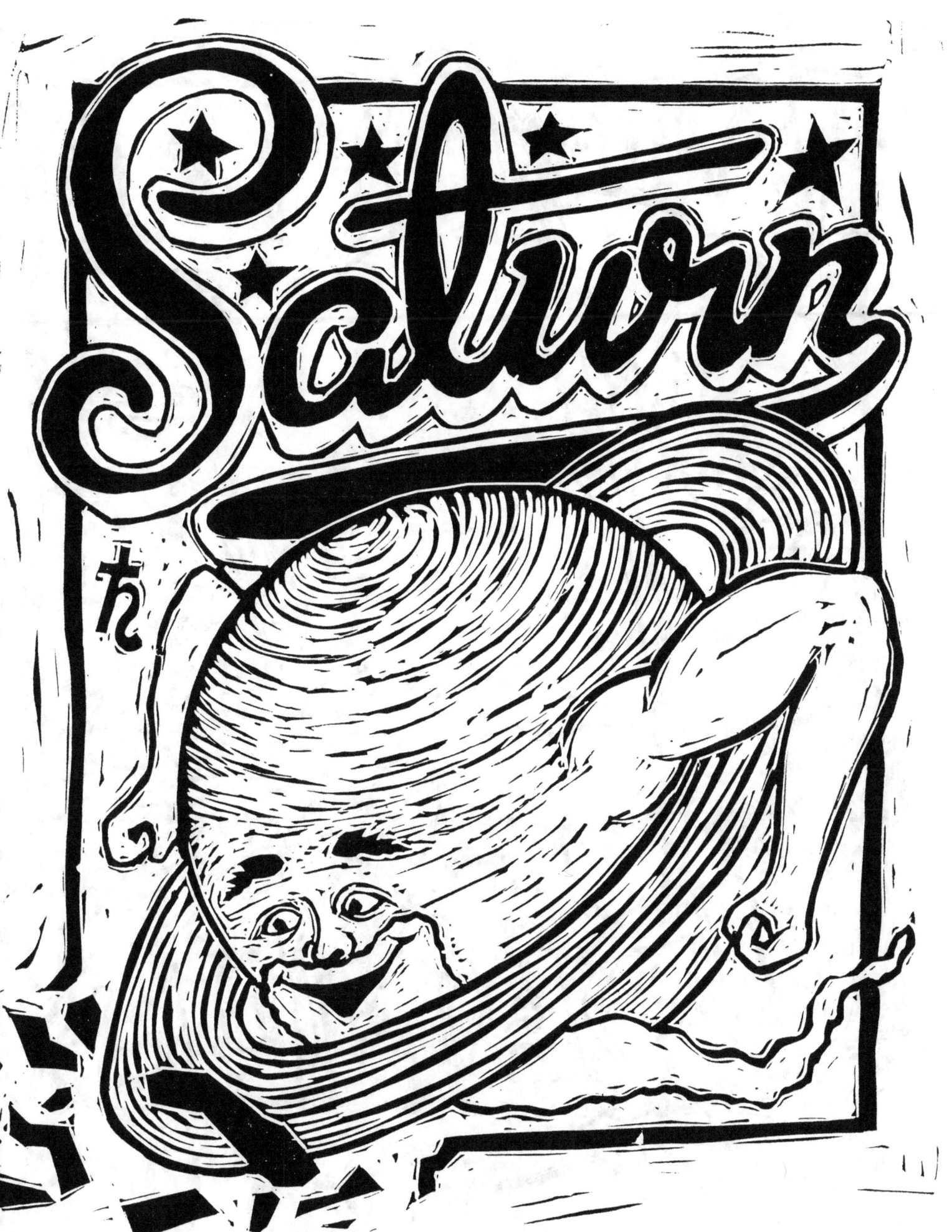

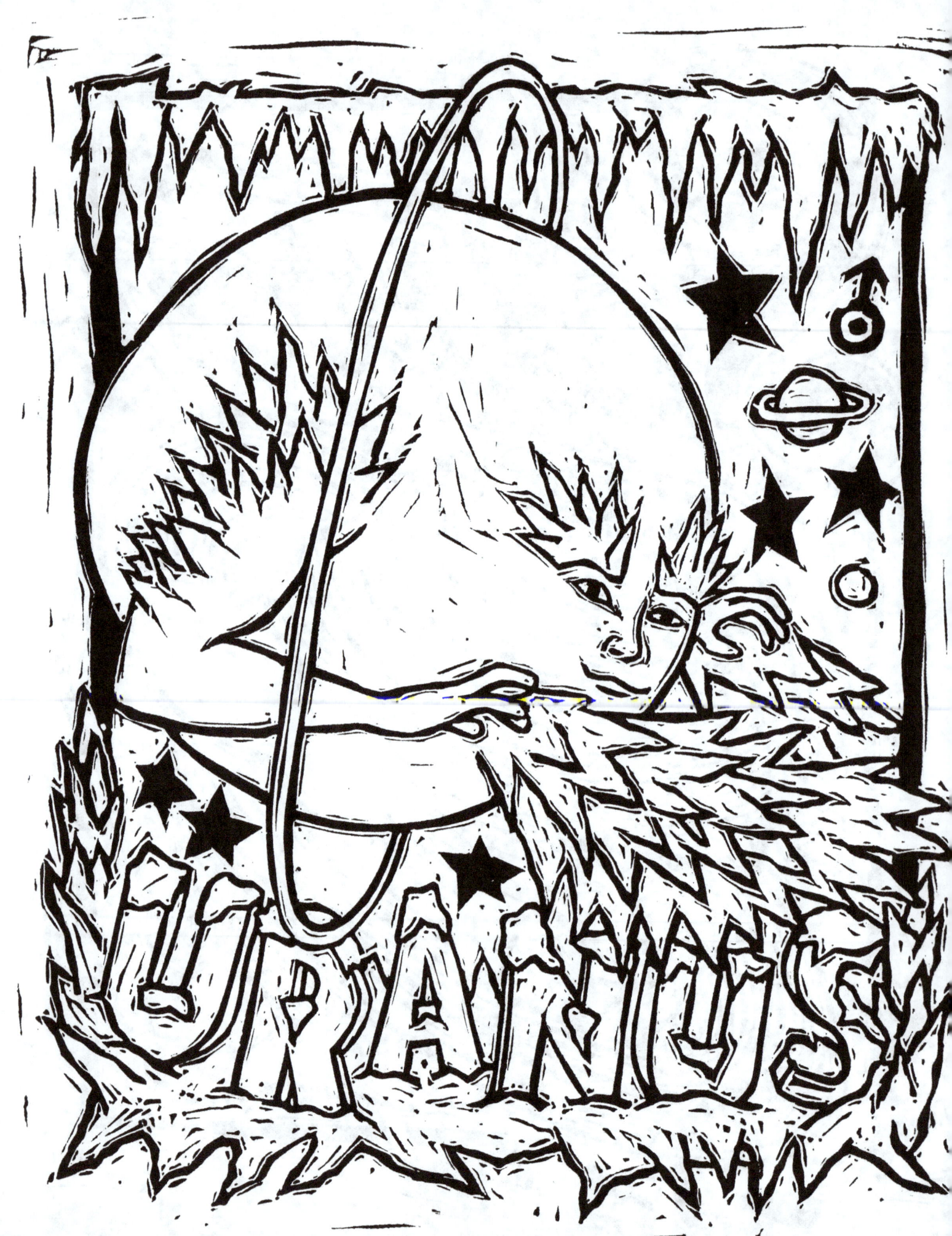

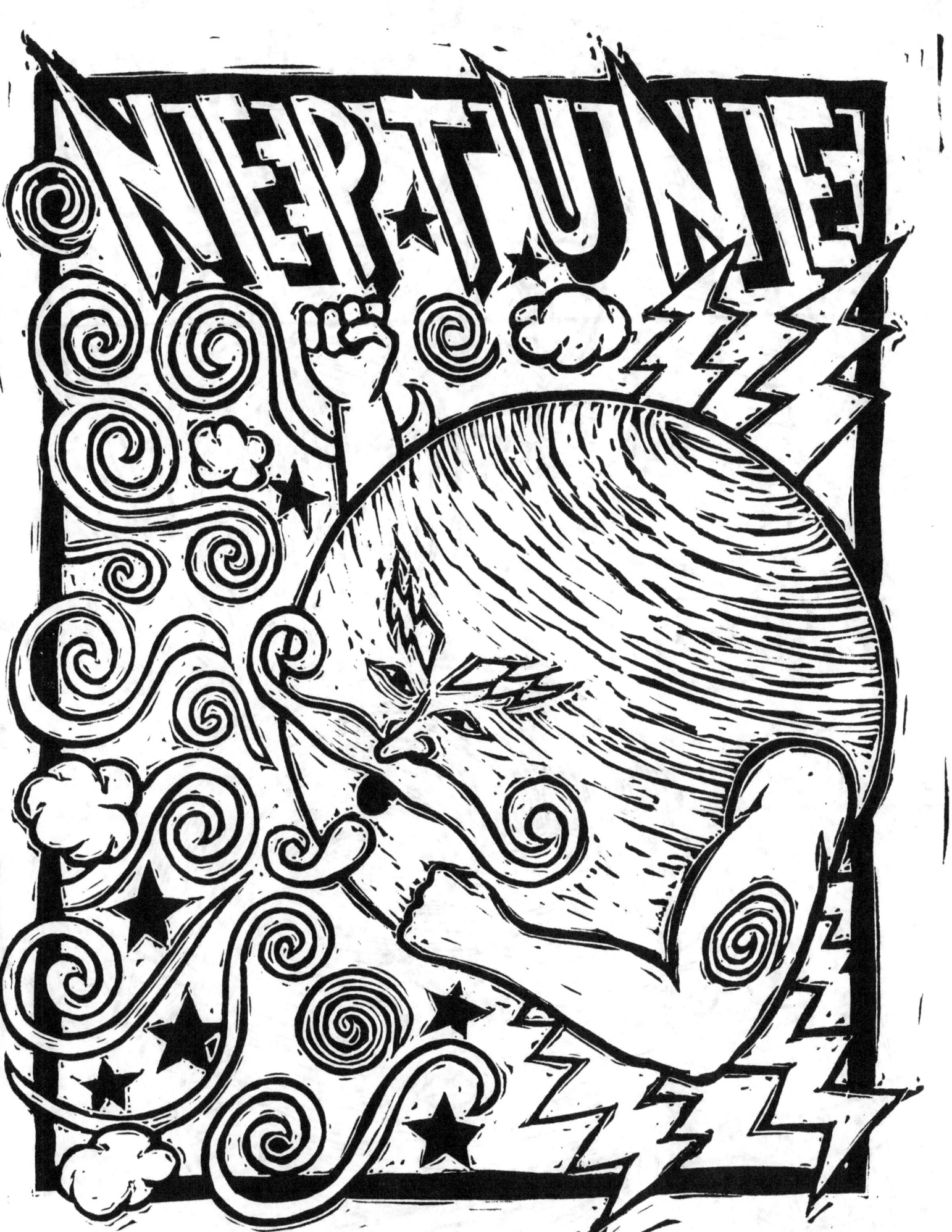

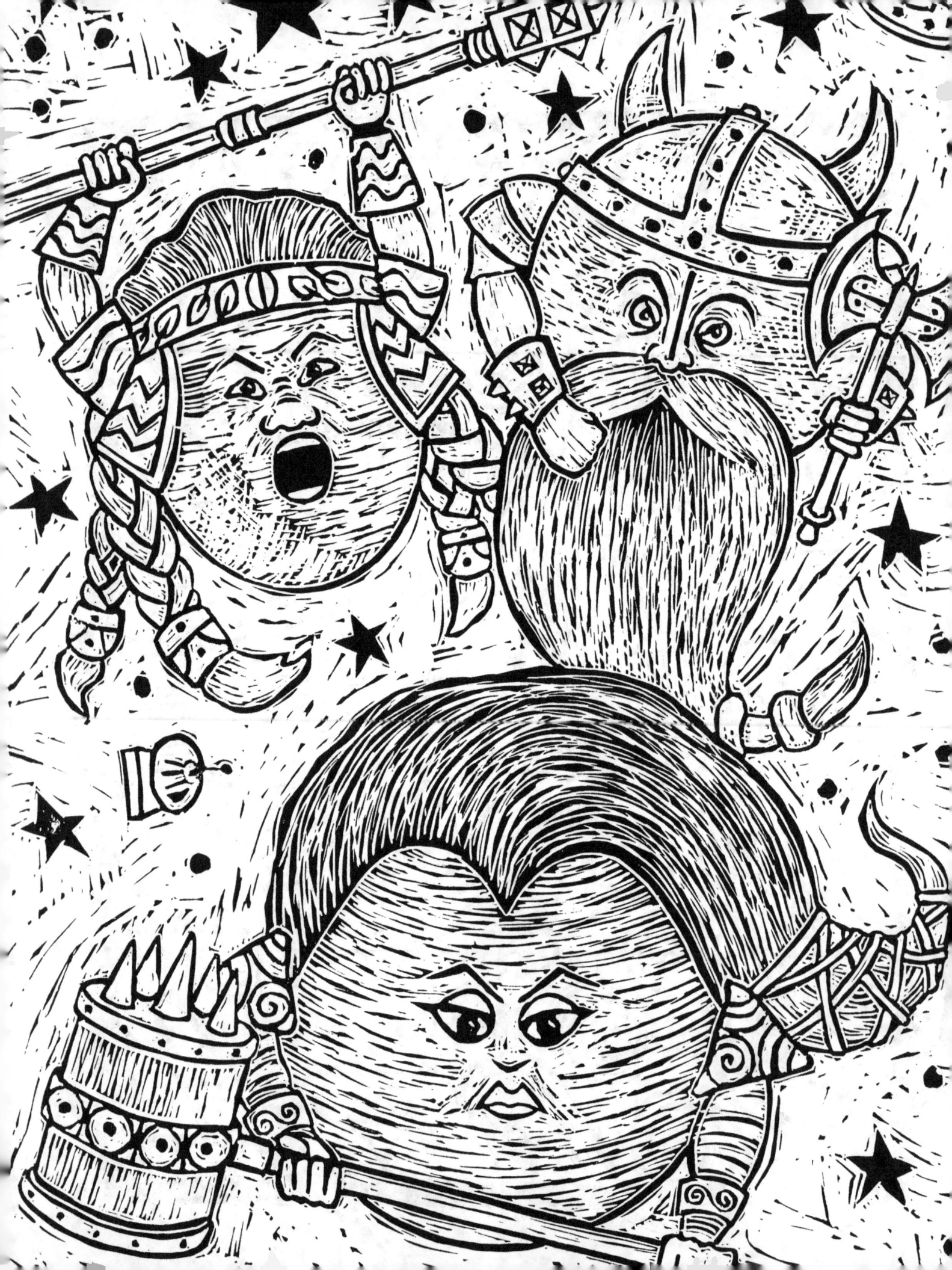

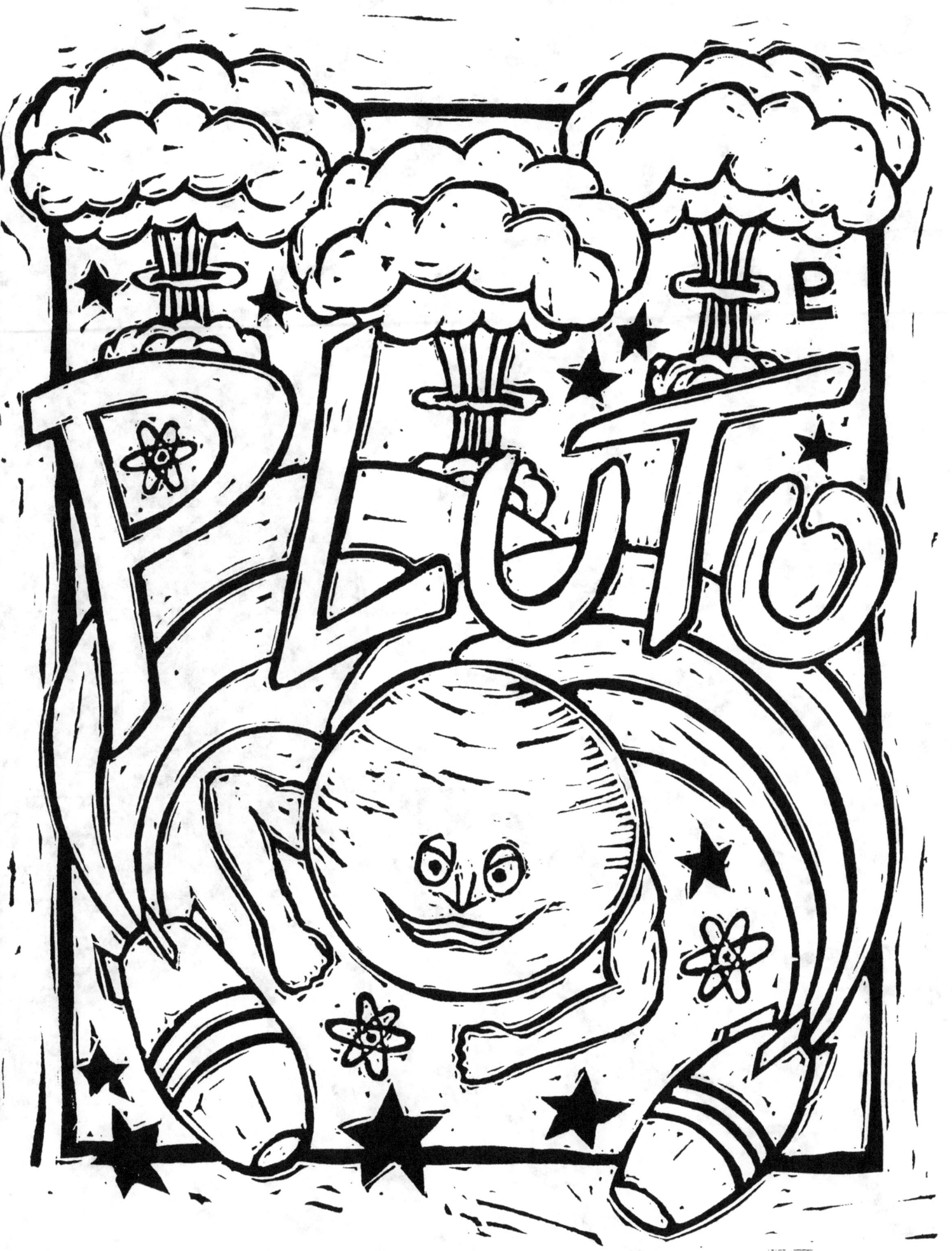

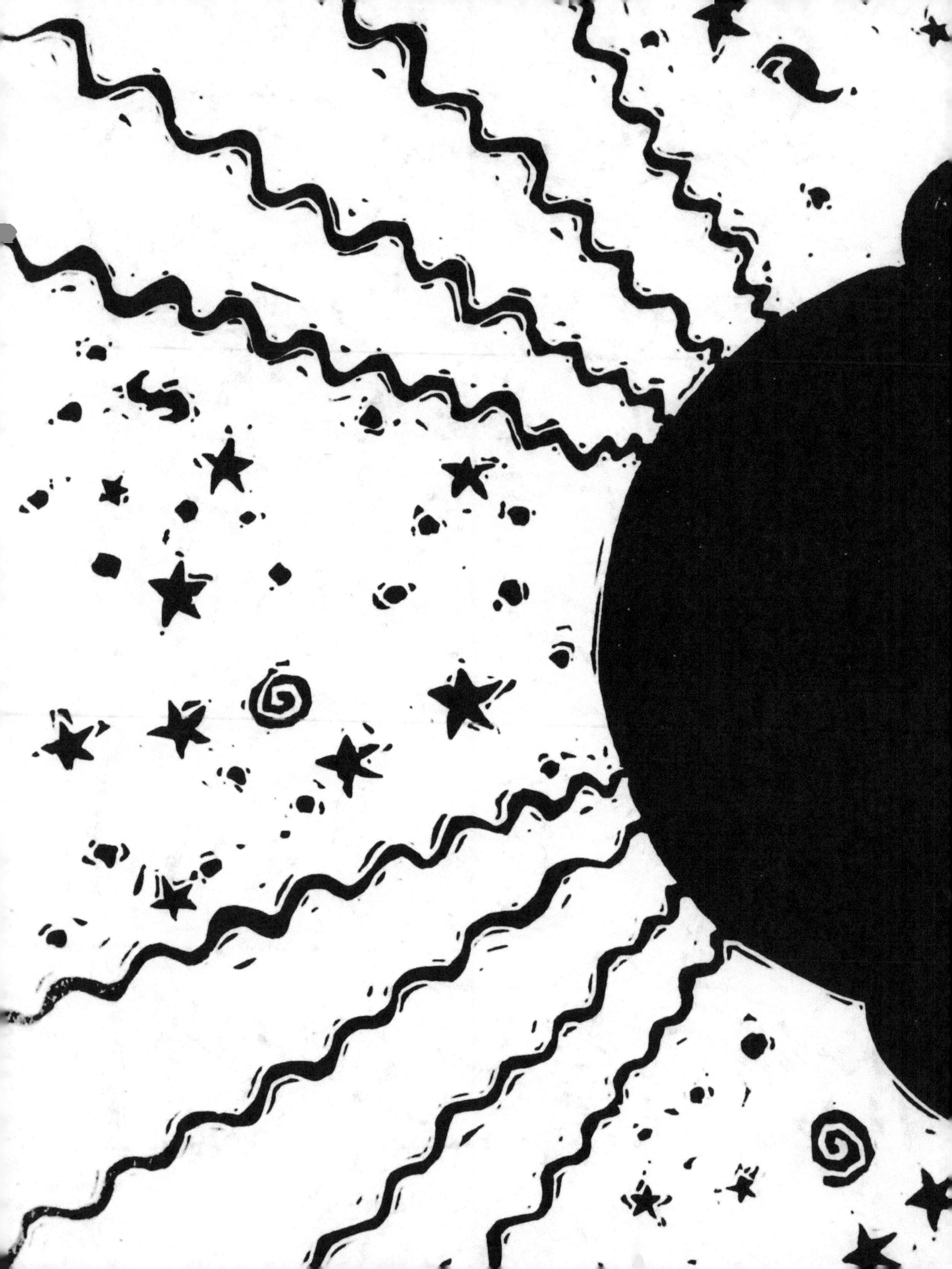

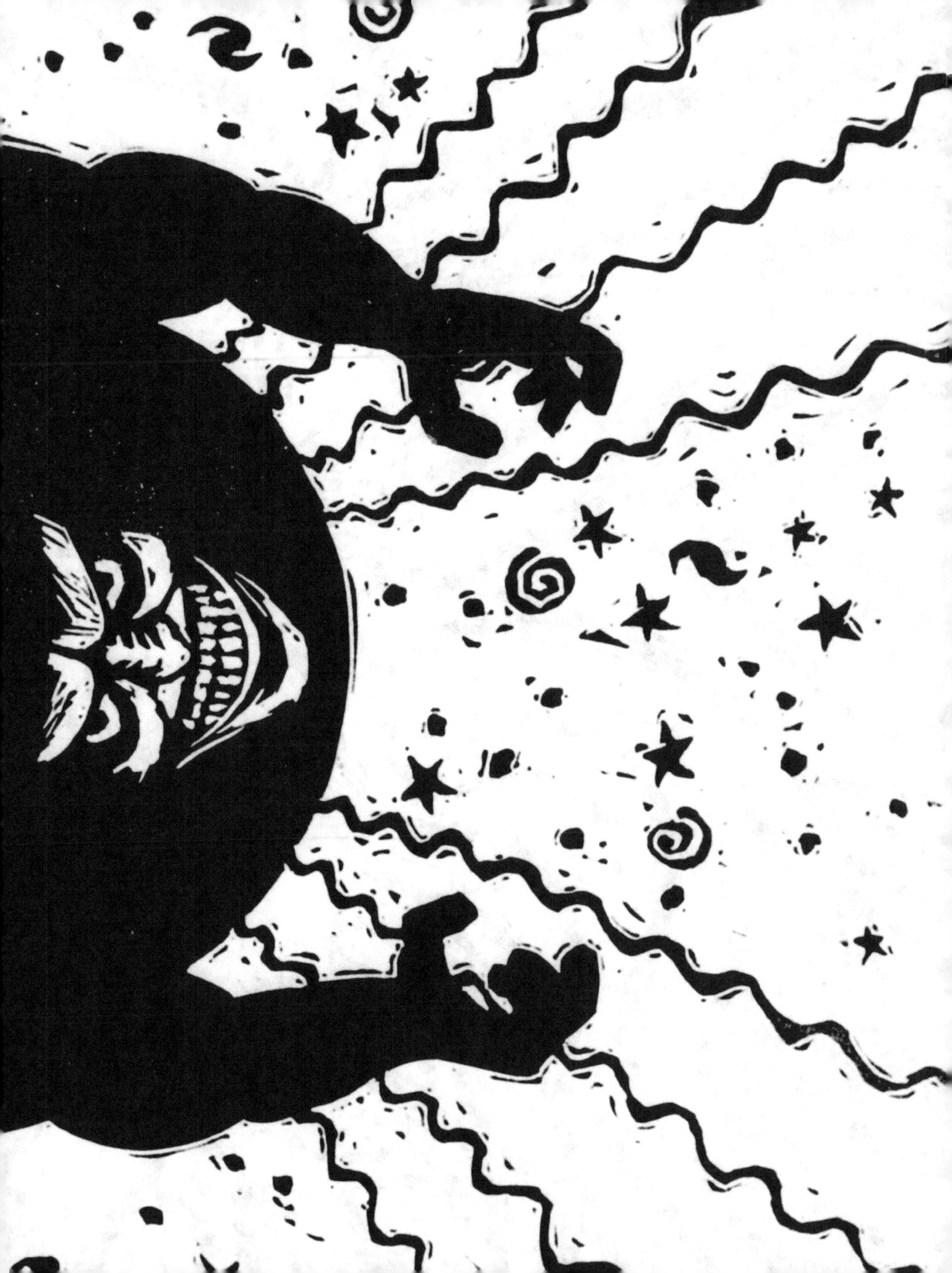

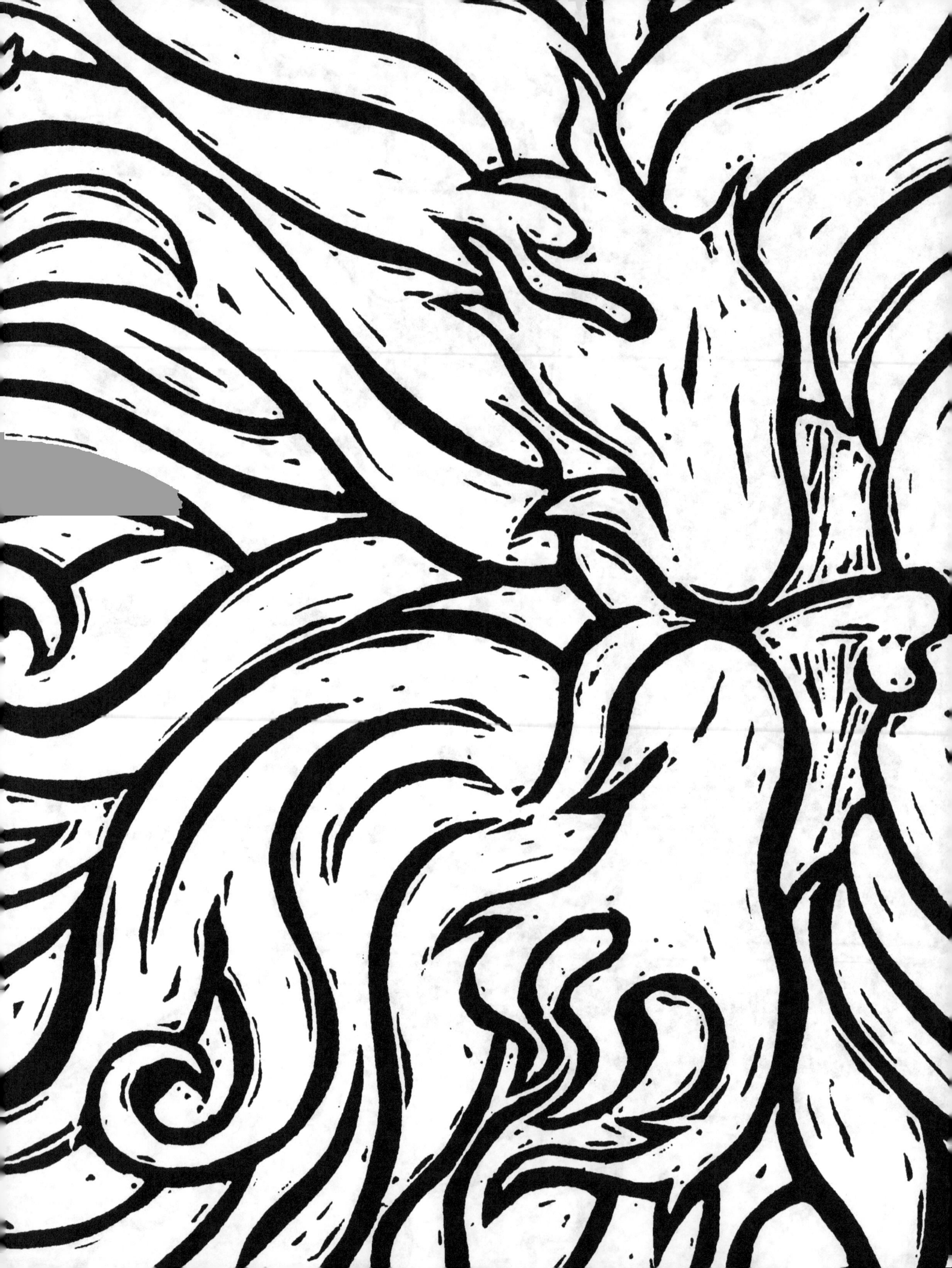

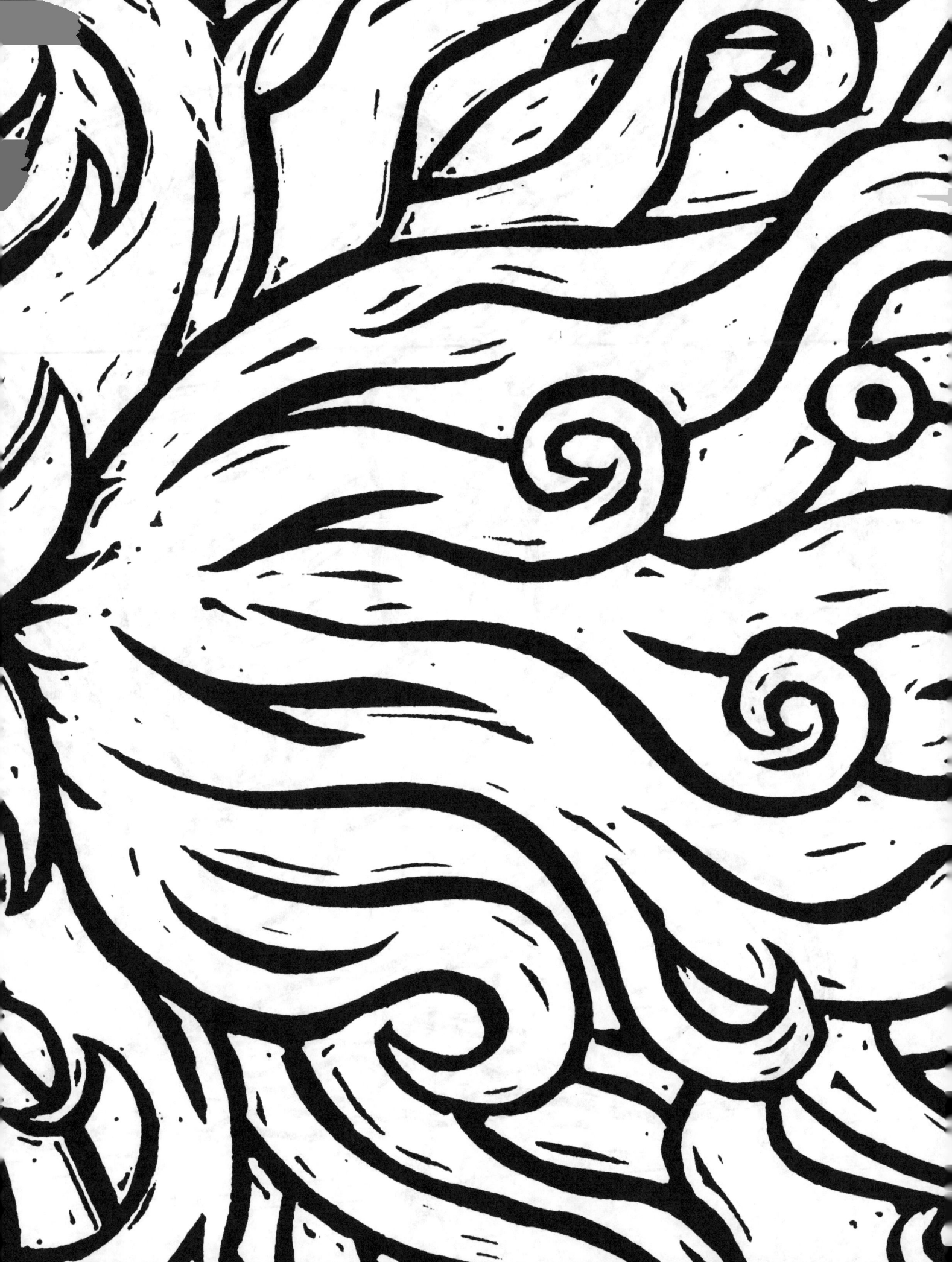

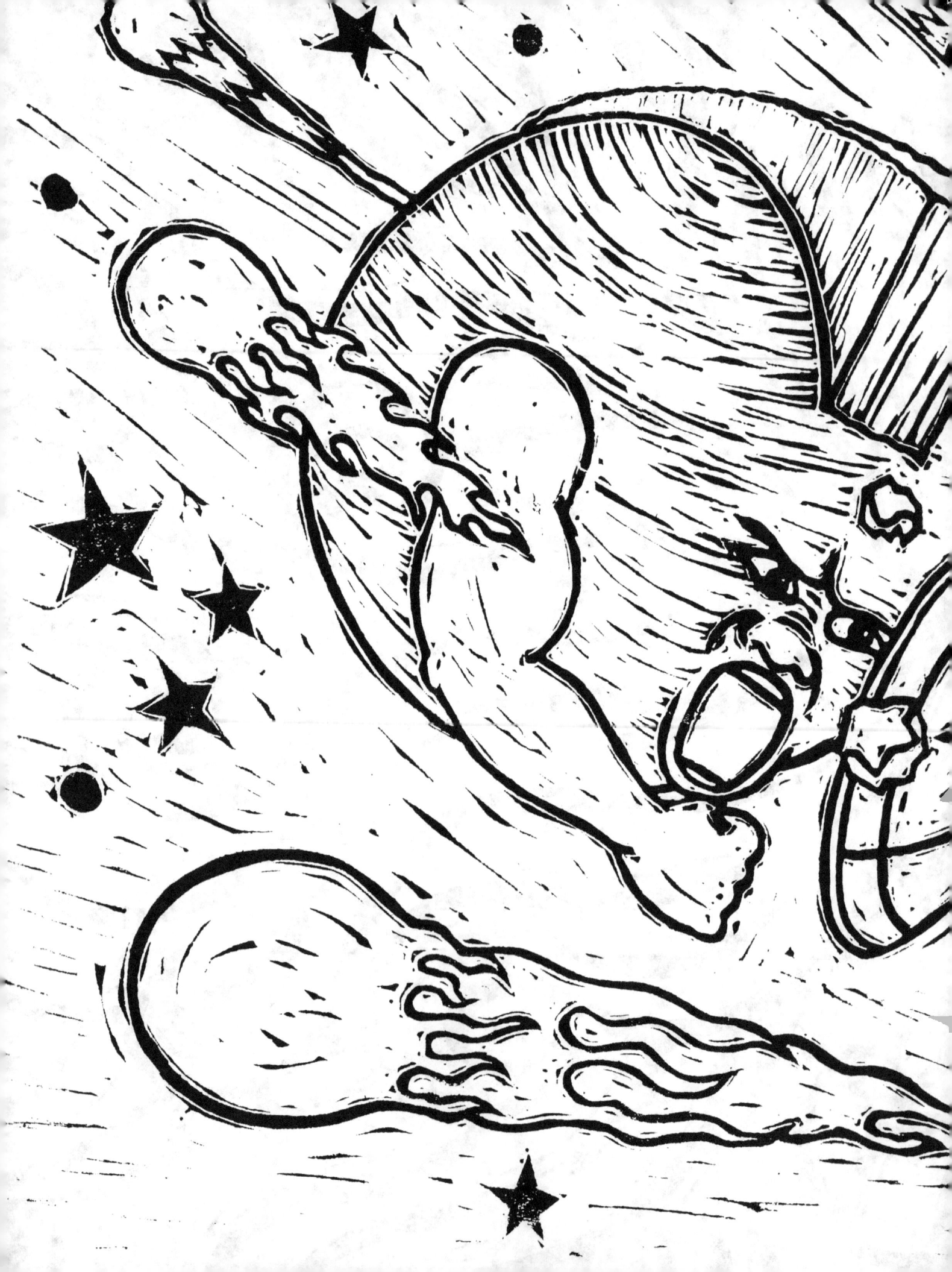

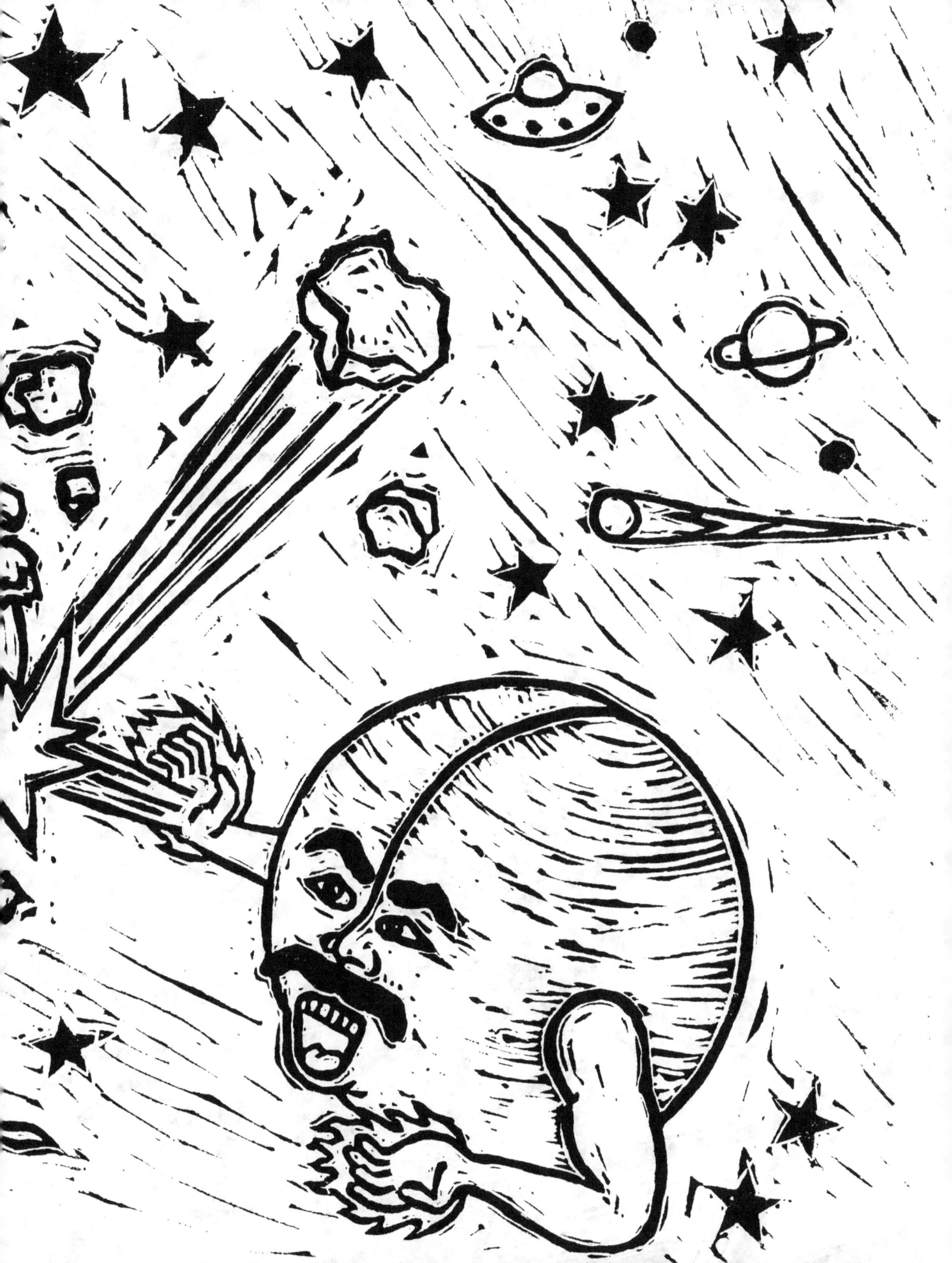

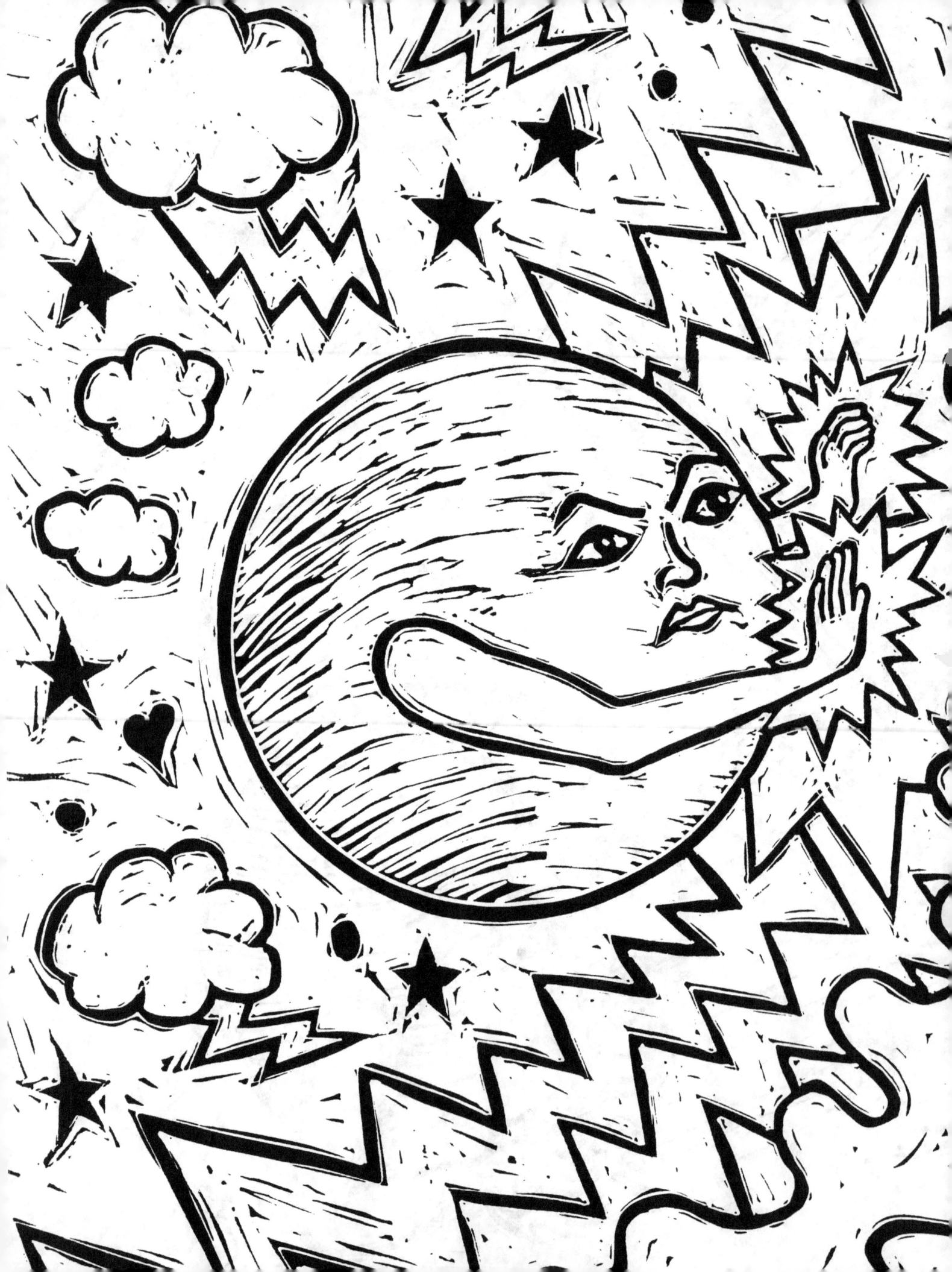

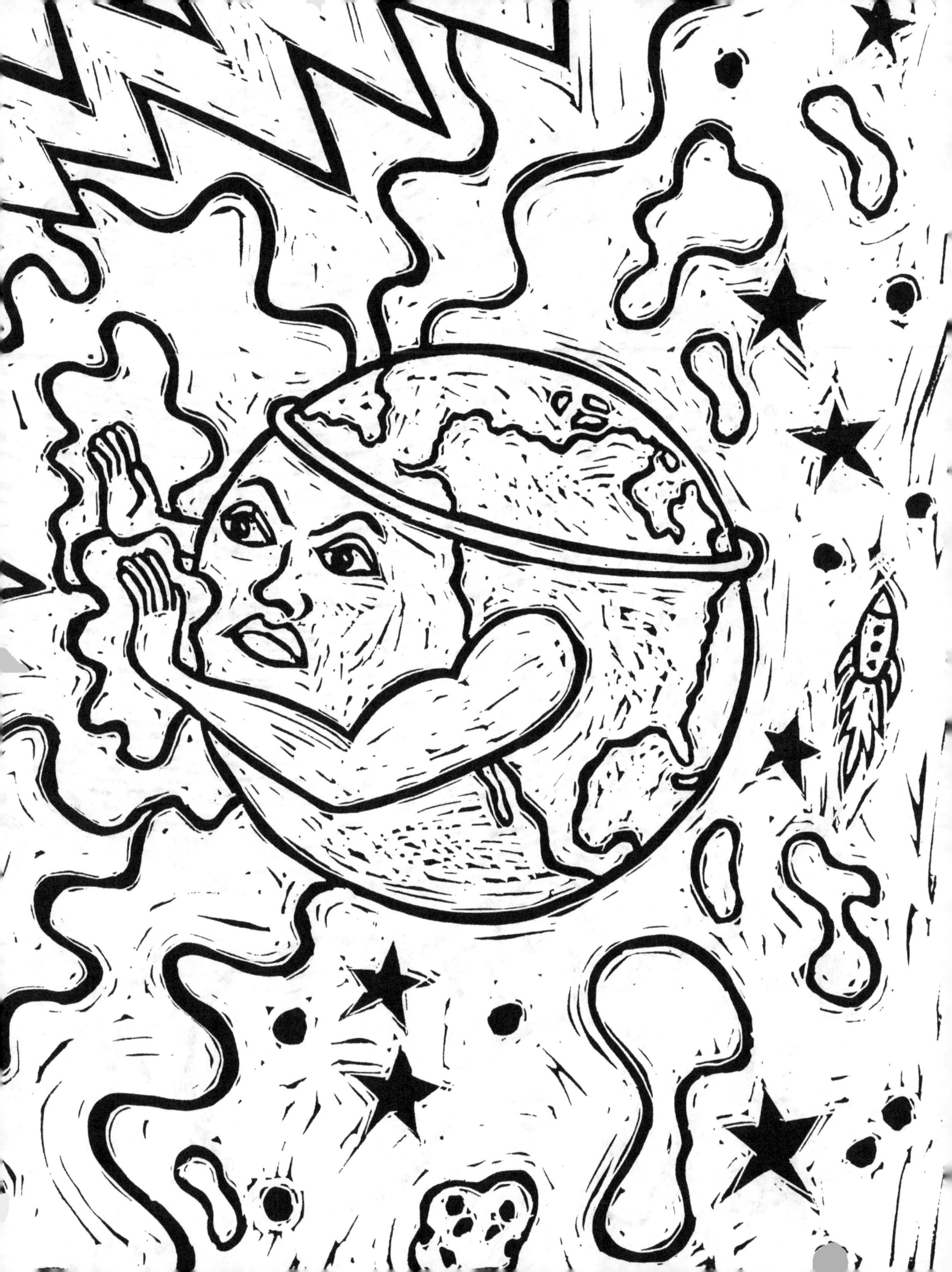

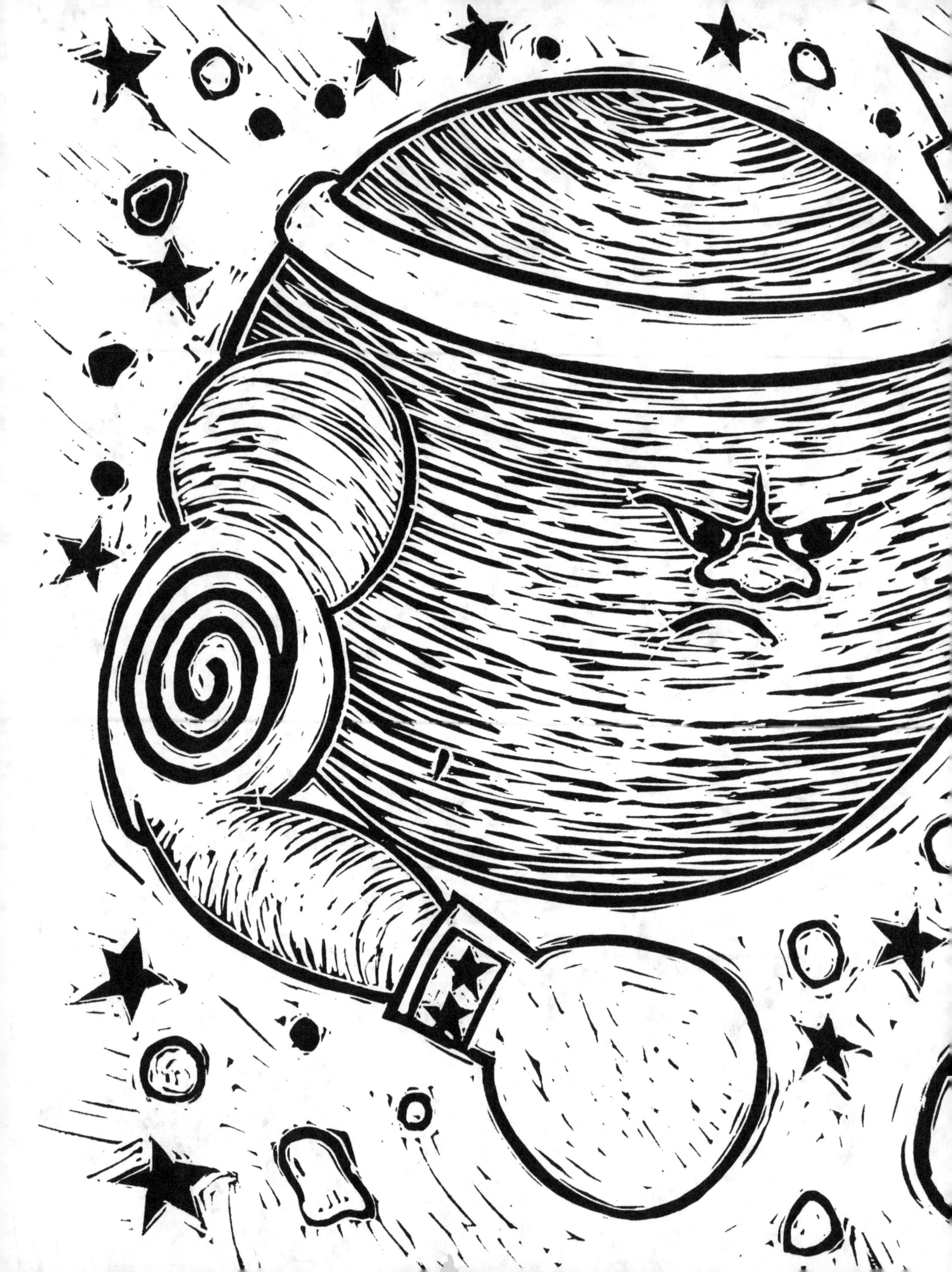

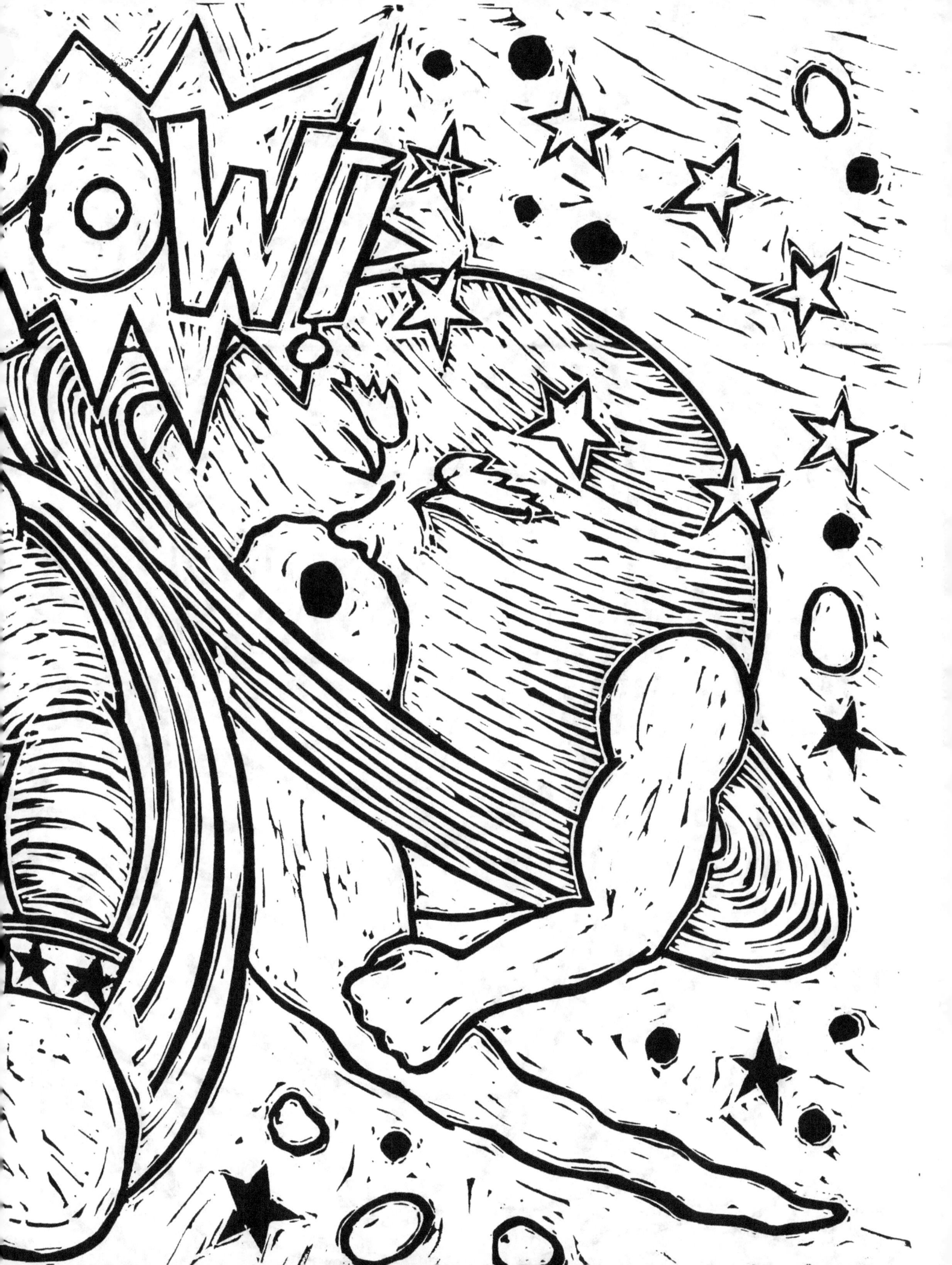

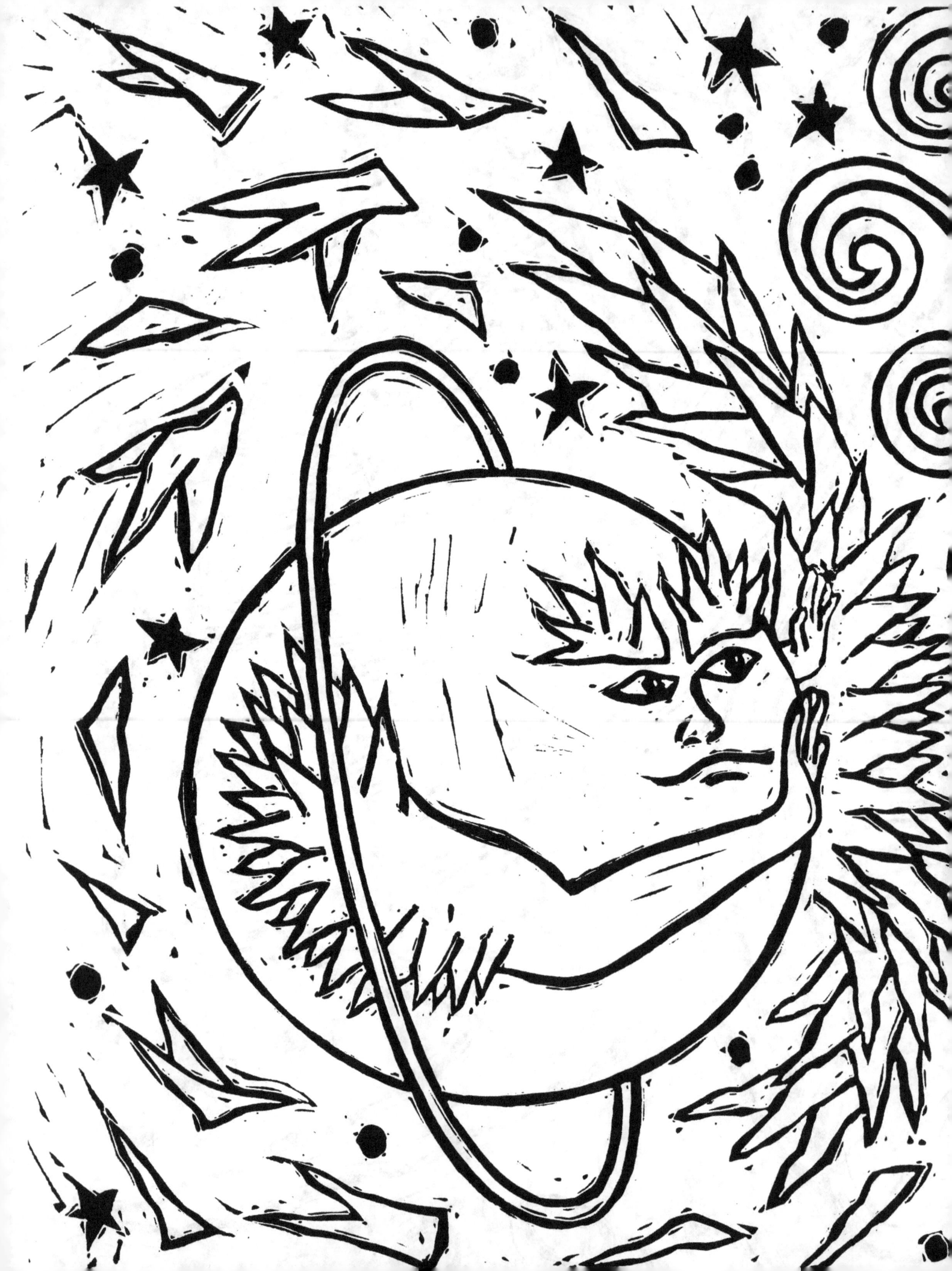

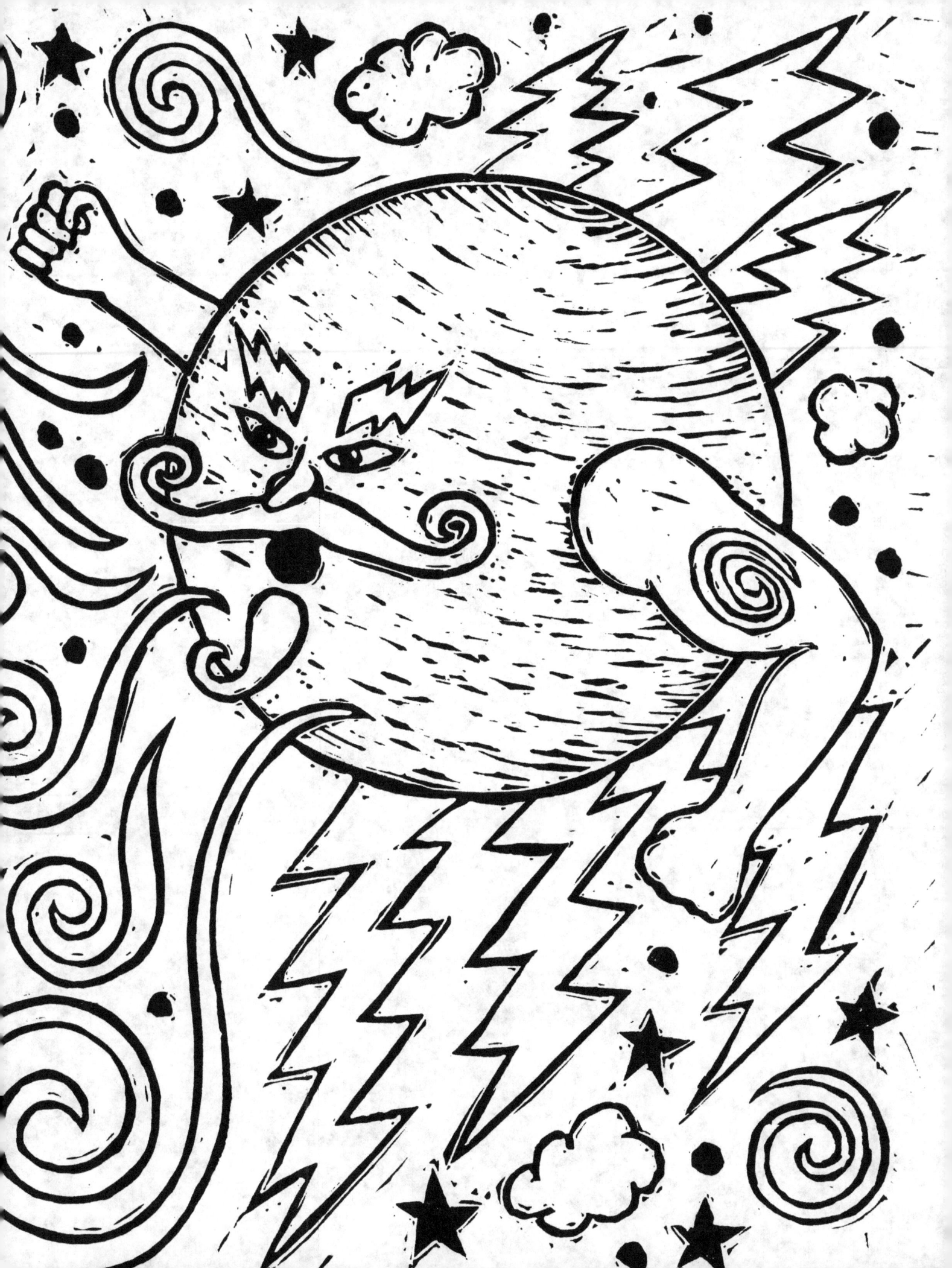

All artwork within this coloring book has been reproduced from original
linocut prints by Jack Wilcox which were made between 2010 and 2016.
Compiled here for the first time in black & white and ready to be colored by you!
By order of appearance each print is titled as follows:

Mercury

Venus

Earth

Earth's Moon

Mars

Ceres

Jupiter

Saturn

Uranus

Neptune

The Dwarf Planets
(Clockwise from top left: Haumea, Makemake, Eris)

Pluto

Planet X

The Sun

Mars vs. Mercury

Venus vs. Earth

Jupiter vs. Saturn

Uranus vs. Neptune

jackwilcoxart.com